MW01144942

A SPECIAL THANK YOU

Gratitude for little ones

written by COLIN DOMBROSKI + illustrated by ALEJANDRO MESA

◆ FriesenPress

Suite 300 – 990 Fort St
Victoria, BC, V8V 3K2
Canada

www.friesenpress.com

Copyright © 2021 by Colin Dombroski
First Edition – 2021

All rights reserved.

No part of this publication may be reproduced in any
form, or by any means, electronic or mechanical, including
photocopying, recording, or any information browsing,
storage, or retrieval system, without permission in writing
from FriesenPress.

ISBN
978-1-5255-9992-7 (Hardcover)
978-1-5255-9991-0 (Paperback)
978-1-5255-9993-4 (eBook)

1. Juvenile Nonfiction, Social Topics, Values & Virtues

Distributed to the trade by The Ingram Book Company

To Lander and Adellaine,

You amaze me every single day.
I love you both to the moon and dinosaurs.

Dad

Your life is so special, in all kinds of ways.
Your family and friends help you
through the days.

A "thank you" will make them
as happy as can be.
How could you thank them?
Turn the pages to see.

Let's start with thinking of Mom
and Dad.
How could you thank them
for a special day you've all had?

A special thank you doesn't have to be grand.
Sometimes it's as simple as holding a hand.

While looking the person right in the eyes,
a "thank you" is special no matter the size.

Your teachers and classmates
all helped with your work.
Having their guidance was such a huge perk!

Finishing a task on your own made you grin.
Now, remember those people
who helped with your win?

Your friends like to see you succeed,
whether counting to ten or learning to read.

A cheerful "thank you" is just
what you need to show your pals
you appreciate their kind deed!

To the people who help you with something you share,
giving you their time is how they show you they care.

It doesn't matter if they are forty or eight,
a special thank you will make them feel great!

Special thank you's are awesome,
no matter the grade.
We're here to help one another,
because we're community made.

About the Author

Colin Dombroski is a husband and father of two. As many parents know, teaching children manners is an important and constant lesson. But, for Colin, it means more than just being polite. It's about recognizing our community and the role they play in our lives. It's about gratitude, and the joy that practicing gratitude can bring to our lives. It's about rewriting our outlook.

Colin lives in London, Ontario with his wife, Cynthia; his children, Lander and Adellaine; and their dogs, Nori and Everest. They love to adventure together and say, "thank you!"

CPSIA information can be obtained
at www.ICGtesting.com
Printed in the USA
LVHW070915061121
702610LV00019B/901